ANOINTED AND SENT

Anointed and Sent

Reflections of Gratitude and Praise for the Priesthood

Pope Francis

Paulist Press
New York / Mahwah, NJ

Cover image by Rudchenko / Dreamstime.com
Cover design by Tamian Wood
Book design by Lynn Else

Library of Congress Cataloging-in-Publication Data
Names: Francis, Pope, 1936– author.
Title: Anointed and sent : reflections of gratitude and praise for the priesthood / Pope Francis.
Other titles: Sermons. Selections. English
Description: New York : Paulist Press, 2020. | Summary: "This work consists of Pope Francis' Chrism Mass homilies delivered to priests of the Diocese of Rome (and worldwide) from 2013 to the present. Also included is the pope's letter on the occasion of the feast of St. John Vianney, the patron saint of priests. Themes include priestly joy and service, and the need for greater communion with Jesus in order to strengthen one's ministry; the question of priestly reform and renewal is addressed"— Provided by publisher.
Identifiers: LCCN 2019043717 (print) | LCCN 2019043718 (ebook) | ISBN 9780809155149 (paperback) | ISBN 9781587689123 (ebook)
Subjects: LCSH: Priesthood—Catholic Church—Sermons. | Pastoral theology—Catholic Church—Sermons. | Clergy—Office—Sermons.
Classification: LCC BX1913 .F7313 2020 (print) | LCC BX1913 (ebook) | DDC 262/.1—dc23
LC record available at https://lccn.loc.gov/2019043717
LC ebook record available at https://lccn.loc.gov/2019043718

ISBN 978-0-8091-5514-9 (paperback)
ISBN 978-1-58768-912-3 (e-book)

Published in North America by Paulist Press
997 Macarthur Boulevard
Mahwah, New Jersey 07430
www.paulistpress.com

Printed and bound in the
United States of America

Contents

Preface

Brothers in Christ,

St. Pope Paul VI wrote, "If a bishop were to concentrate his most constant understanding, patient and cordial attention on the formation, the assistance, the listening to, the guidance, the instruction, the exhortation and the encouragement of his clergy, he would have well employed his time, his heart and his activity."

As Bishop of Rome, and pastor of the universal Church, Pope Francis has concentrated his attention, encouragement, and gratitude to priests in this book. Comprised of his homilies given at the Chrism Mass in his Diocese of Rome and his universal letter to priests given on the Feast of St. John Vianney, Pope Francis opens his heart to you with words of inspiration, gratitude, direction, and challenge. It is his fervent hope that as you read and reflect on his words, the Holy Spirit will stir into flame the gifts of service and joy bestowed on you by the grace of ordination.

The Holy Father's words are a most welcome gift, coming as they do at a particularly difficult time for the Church. Amid the pain, ugliness, and anger, it is possible for the Church, and especially those who are priests, to fall into despair—the opposite of hope. Instead, the Holy Father reminds us that we must never lose sight of those "luminous moments when we experienced the Lord's call to devote ourselves to his service." That sort of memory recalls the many moments of gratitude and encouragement offered to us from the Lord and from others. While working to protect all of God's people, especially the innocent and vulnerable from the evil abuse of power, we should not become blind to how the joy and hope of Christ "are constantly born anew." Speaking as a priest and bishop of the United States, I thank the Holy Father and recommend his words to your prayerful reflection.

In Christ Our Redeemer,

Cardinal Joseph W. Tobin, CSsR
Archbishop of Newark

Introduction

"Let us not grow discouraged!":
A Renewal of Priestly Holiness

Letter of His Holiness to Priests on the 160th Anniversary of the Holy Curé of Ars, St. John Vianney, Rome, August 4, 2019

To my Brother Priests
Dear Brothers,

A hundred and sixty years have passed since the death of the holy Curé of Ars, whom Pope Pius XI proposed as the patron saint of parish priests throughout the world.[1] On this, his feast day, I write this letter not only to parish priests but to all of you, my brother priests, who have quietly "left all behind" in order to immerse yourselves in the daily life of your communities. Like the Curé of Ars, you serve "in the trenches," bearing the burden of the day and the heat (cf. Matt 20:12), confronting an endless variety of situations in your effort to care for and accompany God's people. I want to say a word to each of you who, often without fanfare and at personal cost, amid weariness, infirmity and sorrow, carry out your mission of service to God and to your people. Despite the hardships of the journey, you are writing the finest pages of the priestly life.

Some time ago, I shared with the Italian bishops my worry that, in more than a few places, our priests feel themselves attacked and blamed for crimes they did not commit. I mentioned that priests need to find in their bishop an older brother and a father who reassures them in these difficult times, encouraging and supporting them along the way.[2]

As an older brother and a father, I too would like in this letter *to thank you* in the name of the holy and faithful People of God for all that you do for them, and *to encourage you never* to forget the words that the Lord spoke with great love to us on the day of our ordination. Those words are the source of our joy: "I no longer call you servants…I call you friends" (John 15:15).[3]

PAIN: "I HAVE SEEN THE SUFFERING OF MY PEOPLE" (EXOD 3:7)

In these years, we have become more attentive to the cry, often silent and suppressed, of our brothers and sisters who were victims of the abuse of power, the abuse of conscience and sexual abuse on the part of ordained ministers. This has been a time of great suffering in the lives of those who experienced such abuse, but also in the lives of their families and of the entire People of God.

As you know, we are firmly committed to carrying out the reforms needed to encourage from the outset a culture of pastoral care, so that the culture of abuse will have no room to develop, much less continue. This task is neither quick nor easy: it demands commitment on the part of all. If in the past, omission may itself have been a kind of response, today we desire conversion, transparency, sincerity and solidarity with victims to become our concrete way of moving forward. This in turn will help make us all the more attentive to every form of human suffering.[4]

This pain has also affected priests. I have seen it in the course of my pastoral visits in my own diocese and elsewhere, in my meetings and personal conversations with priests. Many have shared with me their outrage at what happened and their frustration that "for all their hard work, they have to face the damage that was done, the suspicion and uncertainty to which it has given rise, and the doubts, fears and disheartenment felt by more than a few."[5] I have received many letters from priests expressing those feelings. At the same time, I am comforted by my meetings with pastors who recognize and share the pain and suffering of the victims and of the People of God, and have tried to find words and actions capable of inspiring hope.

Without denying or dismissing the harm caused by some of our brothers, it would be unfair not to express our gratitude to all those priests who faithfully and generously spend their lives in the service of others (cf. 2 Cor 12:15). They embody a spiritual fatherhood capable of weeping with those who weep. Countless priests make of their lives a work of mercy in areas or situations that are often hostile, isolated or ignored, even at the risk of their lives. I acknowledge and appreciate your courageous and steadfast example; in these times of turbulence, shame and pain, you demonstrate that you have joyfully put your lives on the line for the sake of the Gospel.[6]

I am convinced that, to the extent that we remain faithful to God's will, these present times of ecclesial purification will make us more joyful and humble, and prove, in the not distant future, very fruitful. "Let us not grow discouraged! The Lord is purifying his Bride and converting all of us to himself. He is letting us be put to the test in order to make us realize that without him we are simply dust. He is rescuing us from hypocrisy, from the spirituality of appearances. He is breathing forth his Spirit in order to restore the beauty of his Bride, caught in adultery. We can benefit from rereading the sixteenth chapter of Ezekiel. It is the history of the Church, and each of us can say it is our history too. In the end, through your sense of shame, you will continue to act as a shepherd. Our humble repentance, expressed in silent tears before these atrocious sins and the unfathomable grandeur of God's forgiveness, is the beginning of a renewal of our holiness."[7]

GRATITUDE: "I DO NOT CEASE TO GIVE THANKS FOR YOU" (EPH 1:16)

Vocation, more than our own choice, is a response to the Lord's unmerited call. We do well to return constantly to those passages of the Gospel where we see Jesus praying, choosing and calling others "to be with him, and to be sent out to proclaim the message" (Mark 3:14).

Here I think of a great master of the priestly life in my own country, Father Lucio Gera. Speaking to a group of priests at a turbulent time in Latin America, he told them: "Always, but especially in times of trial, we need to return to those luminous moments when we experienced the Lord's call to devote our lives to his service." I myself like to call this "the deuteronomic memory of our vocation"; it makes each of us go back "to that blazing light with which God's grace touched me at the start of the journey. From that flame, I can light a fire for today and every day, and bring heat and light to my brothers and sisters. That flame ignites a humble joy, a joy which sorrow and distress cannot dismay, a good and gentle joy."[8]

One day, each of us spoke up and said "yes," a "yes" born and developed in the heart of the Christian community thanks to those "saints next door"[9] who showed us by their simple faith that it was worthwhile committing ourselves completely to the Lord and his kingdom. A "yes" whose implications were so momentous that often we find it hard to imagine all the goodness that it continues to produce. How beautiful it is when an elderly priest sees or is visited by those children—now adults—whom he baptized long ago and who now gratefully introduce a family of their own! At times like this, we realize that we were anointed to anoint others, and that God's anointing never disappoints. I am led to say with the Apostle: "I do not cease to give thanks for you" (cf. Eph 1:16) and for all the good that you have done.

Amid trials, weakness and the consciousness of our limitations, "the worst temptation of all is to keep brooding over our troubles"[10] for then we lose our perspective, our good judgement and our courage. At those times, it is important—I would even say crucial—to cherish the memory of the Lord's presence in our lives and his merciful gaze, which inspired us to put our lives on the line for him and for his People. And to find the strength to persevere and, with the Psalmist, to raise our own song of praise, "for his mercy endures forever" (Ps 136).

Gratitude is always a powerful weapon. Only if we are able to contemplate and feel genuine gratitude for all those ways we have experienced God's love, generosity, solidarity and trust, as well as his forgiveness, patience, forbearance and compassion, will we allow the Spirit to grant us the freshness that can renew (and not simply patch up) our life and mission. Like Peter on the morning of the miraculous draught of fishes, may we let the recognition of all the blessings we have received awaken in us the amazement and gratitude that can enable us to say: "Depart from me, Lord, for I am a sinful man" (Luke 5:8). Only then to hear the Lord repeat his summons: "Do not be afraid; from now on you will be fishers of men." (Luke 5:10). "For his mercy endures forever."

Dear brother priests, I thank you for your fidelity to the commitments you have made. It is a sign that, in a society and culture that glorifies the ephemeral, there are still people unafraid to make lifelong promises. In effect, we show that we continue to believe in God, who has never broken his covenant, despite our having broken it countless times. In this way, we celebrate the fidelity of God, who continues to trust us, to believe in us and to count on us, for all our sins and failings, and who invites us to be faithful in turn. Realizing that we hold this treasure in earthen vessels (cf. 2 Cor 4:7), we know that the Lord triumphs through weakness (cf. 2 Cor 12:9). He continues to sustain us and to renew his call, repaying us a hundredfold (cf. Mark 10:29–30). "For his mercy endures forever."

Thank you for the joy with which you have offered your lives, revealing a heart that over the years has refused to become closed and bitter, but has grown daily in love for God and his people. A heart that, like good wine, has not turned sour but become richer with age. "For his mercy endures forever."

Thank you for working to strengthen the bonds of fraternity and friendship with your brother priests and your bishop, providing one another with support and encouragement, caring for those who are ill, seeking out those who keep apart, visiting the elderly and drawing from their wisdom, sharing with one another and learning to laugh and cry together. How much we need this! But thank you too for your faithfulness and perseverance in undertaking difficult missions, or for those times when you have had to call a brother priest to order. "For his mercy endures forever."

Thank you for your witness of persistence and patient endurance (in Greek *hypomoné*) in pastoral ministry. Often, with the *parrhesía* of the shepherd,[11] we find ourselves arguing with the Lord in prayer, as Moses did in courageously interceding for the people (cf. Num 14:13–19; Exod 32:30–32; Deut 9:18–21). "For his mercy endures forever."

Thank you for celebrating the Eucharist each day and for being merciful shepherds in the Sacrament of Reconciliation, neither rigorous nor lax, but deeply concerned for your people and accompanying them on their journey of conversion to the new life that the Lord bestows on us all. We know that on the ladder of mercy we can descend to the depths of our human condition—including weakness and sin—and at the same time experience the heights of divine perfection: "Be merciful as the Father is merciful."[12] In this way, we are "capable of warming people's hearts, walking at their side in the dark, talking with them and even entering into their night and their darkness, without losing our way."[13] "For his mercy endures forever."

Thank you for anointing and fervently proclaiming to all, "in season and out of season" (cf. 2 Tim 4:2) the Gospel of Jesus Christ, probing the heart of your community "in order to discover where its desire for God is alive and ardent, as well as where that dialogue, once loving, has been thwarted and is now barren."[14] "For his mercy endures forever."

Thank you for the times when, with great emotion, you embraced sinners, healed wounds, warmed hearts and showed the tenderness and compassion of the Good Samaritan (cf. Luke 10:25–27). Nothing is more necessary than this: accessibility, closeness, readiness to draw near to the flesh of our suffering brothers and sisters. How powerful is the example of a priest who makes himself present and does not flee the wounds of his brothers and sisters![15] It mirrors the heart of a shepherd who has developed a spiritual taste for being one with his people,[16] a pastor who never forgets that he has come from them and that by serving them he will find and express his most pure and complete identity. This in turn will lead to adopting a simple and austere way of life, rejecting privileges that have nothing to do with the Gospel. "For his mercy endures forever."

Finally, let us give thanks for the holiness of the faithful People of God, whom we are called to shepherd and through whom the Lord also shepherds and cares for us. He blesses us with the gift of contemplating that faithful People "in those parents who raise their children with immense love, in those men and women who work hard to support their families, in the sick, in elderly religious who never lose their smile. In their daily perseverance, I see the holiness of the Church militant."[17] Let us be grateful for each of them, and in their witness find support and encouragement. "For his mercy endures forever."

ENCOURAGEMENT: "I WANT [YOUR] HEARTS TO BE ENCOURAGED" (COL 2:2)

My second great desire is, in the words of Saint Paul, to offer encouragement as we strive to renew our priestly spirit, which is above all the fruit of the working of the Holy Spirit in our lives. Faced with painful experiences, all of us need to be comforted and encouraged. The mission to which we are called does not exempt us from suffering, pain and even misunderstanding.[18] Rather, it requires us to face them squarely and to accept them, so that the Lord can transform them and conform us more closely to himself. "Ultimately, the lack of a heartfelt and prayerful acknowledgment of our limitations prevents grace from working more effectively within us, for no room is left for bringing about the potential good that is part of a sincere and genuine journey of growth."[19]

One good way of testing our hearts as pastors is to ask how we confront suffering. We can often act like the Levite or the priest in the parable, stepping aside and ignoring the injured man (cf. Luke 10:31–32). Or we can draw near in the wrong way, viewing situations in the abstract and taking refuge in commonplaces, such as: "That's life...," or "Nothing can be done." In this way, we yield to an uneasy fatalism. Or else we can draw near with a kind of aloofness that brings only isolation and exclusion. "Like the prophet Jonah, we are constantly tempted to flee to a safe haven. It can have many names: individualism, spiritualism, living in a little world...."[20] Far from making us compassionate, this ends up holding us back from confronting our own wounds, the wounds of others and consequently the wounds of Jesus himself.[21]

Along these same lines, I would mention another subtle and dangerous attitude, which, as Bernanos liked to say, is "the most precious of the devil's potions."[22] It is also the most harmful for those of us who would serve the Lord, for it breeds discouragement, desolation and despair.[23] Disappointment with life, with the Church or with ourselves can tempt us to latch onto a *sweet sorrow* or sadness that the Eastern Fathers called *acedia*. Cardinal Tomáš Špidlík described it in these terms: "If we are assailed by sadness at life, at the company of others or at our own isolation, it is because we lack faith in God's providence and his works....Sadness paralyzes our desire to persevere in our work and prayer; it makes us hard to live with.... The monastic authors who treated this vice at length call it the worst enemy of the spiritual life."[24]

All of us are aware of a sadness that can turn into a habit and lead us slowly to accept evil and injustice by quietly telling us: "It has always been like this." A sadness that stifles every effort at change and conversion by sowing resentment and hostility. "That is no way to live a dignified and fulfilled life; it is not God's will for us, nor is it the life of the Spirit, which has its source in the heart of the risen Christ,"[25] to which we have been called. Dear brothers, when that *sweet sorrow* threatens to take hold of our lives or our communities, without being fearful or troubled, yet with firm resolution, let us together beg the Spirit to "rouse us from our torpor, to free us from our inertia. Let us rethink our usual way of doing things; let us open our eyes and ears, and above all our hearts, so as not to be complacent about things as they are, but unsettled by the living and effective word of the risen Lord."[26]

Let me repeat: in times of difficulty, we all need God's consolation and strength, as well as that of our brothers and sisters. All of us can benefit from the touching words that Saint Paul addressed to his communities: "I pray that you may not lose heart over [my] sufferings" (Eph 3:13), and "I want [your] hearts to be encouraged" (Col 2:22). In this way, we can carry out the mission that the Lord gives us anew each day: to proclaim "good news of great joy for all the people" (Luke 2:10). Not by presenting intellectual theories or moral axioms about the way things ought to be, but as men who in the midst of pain have been transformed and transfigured by the Lord and, like Job, can exclaim: "I knew you then only by hearsay, but now I have seen you with my own eyes" (Job 42:2). Without this foundational experience, all of our hard work will only lead to frustration and disappointment.

In our own lives, we have seen how "with Christ, joy is constantly born anew."[27] Although there are different stages in this experience, we know that, despite our frailties and sins, "with a tenderness which never disappoints, but is always capable of restoring our joy, God makes it possible for us to lift up our heads and start anew."[28] That joy is not the fruit of our own thoughts or decisions, but of the confidence born of knowing the enduring truth of Jesus' words to Peter. At times of uncertainty, remember those words: "I have prayed for you, that your faith may not fail" (Luke 22:32). The Lord is the first to pray and fight for you and for me. And he invites us to enter fully into his own prayer. There may well be moments when we too have to enter into "the prayer of Gethsemane, that most human and dramatic of Jesus' prayers....For there we find supplication, sorrow, anguish and even bewilderment" (Mark 14:33ff.).[29]

We know that it is not easy to stand before the Lord and let his gaze examine our lives, heal our wounded hearts and cleanse our feet of the worldliness accumulated along the way, which now keeps us from moving forward. In prayer, we experience the blessed "insecurity" which reminds us that we are disciples in need of the Lord's help, and which frees us from the promethean tendency of "those who ultimately trust only in their own powers and feel superior to others because they observe certain rules."[30]

Dear brothers, Jesus, more than anyone, is aware of our efforts and our accomplishments, our failures and our mistakes. He is the first to tell us: "Come to me, all you who are weary and are carrying heavy burdens, and I will give you rest. Take my yoke upon you, and learn from me; for I am gentle and humble in heart, and you will find rest for your souls" (Matt 11:28–29).

In this prayer, we know that we are never alone. The prayer of a pastor embraces both the Spirit who cries out "Abba, Father!" (cf. Gal 4:6), and the people who have been entrusted to his care. Our mission and identity can be defined by this dialectic.

The prayer of a pastor is nourished and made incarnate in the heart of God's People. It bears the marks of the sufferings and joys of his people, whom he silently presents to the Lord to be anointed by the gift of the Holy Spirit. This is the hope of a pastor, who with trust and insistence asks the Lord to care for our weakness as individuals and as a people. Yet we should also realize that it is in the prayer of God's People that the heart of a pastor takes flesh and finds its proper place. This sets us free from looking for quick, easy, ready-made answers; it allows the Lord to be the one—not our own recipes and goals—to point out a path of hope. Let us not forget that at the most difficult times in the life of the earliest community, as we read in the Acts of the Apostles, prayer emerged as the true guiding force.

Brothers, let us indeed acknowledge our weaknesses, but also let Jesus transform them and send us forth anew to the mission. Let us never lose the joy of knowing that we are "the sheep of his flock" and that he is our Lord and Shepherd.

For our hearts to be encouraged, we should not neglect the dialectic that determines our identity. First, our relationship with Jesus. Whenever we turn away from Jesus or neglect our relationship with him, slowly but surely our commitment begins to fade and our lamps lose the oil needed to light up our lives (cf. Matt 25:1–13): "Abide in me as I abide in you. Just as the branch cannot bear fruit by itself unless it abides in the vine, neither can you unless you abide in me...because apart from me you can do nothing" (John 15:4–5). In this regard, I would encourage you not to neglect spiritual direction. Look for a brother with whom you can speak, reflect, discuss and discern, sharing with complete trust and openness your journey. A wise brother with whom to share the experience of discipleship. Find him, meet with him and enjoy his guidance, accompaniment and counsel. This is an indispensable aid to carrying out your ministry in obedience to the will of the Father (cf. Heb 10:9) and letting your heart beat with "the mind that was in Christ Jesus" (Phil 2:5). We can profit from the words of Ecclesiastes: "Two are better than one....One will lift up the other; but woe to the one who is alone and falls, and does not have another to help!" (4:9–10).

The other essential aspect of this dialectic is our relationship to our people. Foster that relationship and expand it. Do not withdraw from your people, your presbyterates and your communities, much less seek refuge in closed and elitist groups. Ultimately, this stifles and poisons the soul. A minister whose "heart is encouraged" is a minister always on the move. In our "going forth," we walk "sometimes in front, sometimes in the middle and sometimes behind: in front, in order to guide the community; in the middle, in order to encourage and support, and at the back in order to keep it united, so that no one lags too far behind....There is another reason too: because our people have a 'nose' for things. They sniff out, discover, new paths to take; they have the *sensus fidei* (cf. *Lumen Gentium* 12). What could be more beautiful than this?"[31] Jesus himself is the model of this evangelizing option that leads us to the heart of our people. How good it is for us to see him in his attention to every person! The sacrifice of Jesus on the cross is nothing else but the culmination of that evangelizing style that marked his entire life.

Dear brother priests, the pain of so many victims, the pain of the people of God and our own personal pain, cannot be for naught. Jesus himself has brought this heavy burden to his cross and he now asks us to be renewed in our mission of drawing near to those who suffer, of drawing near without embarrassment to human misery, and indeed to make all these experiences our own, as Eucharist.[32] Our age, marked by old and new wounds, requires us to be builders of relationships and communion, open, trusting and awaiting in hope the newness that the kingdom of God wishes to bring about even today. For it is a kingdom of forgiven sinners called to bear witness to the Lord's ever-present compassion. "For his mercy endures forever."

PRAISE: "MY SOUL PROCLAIMS THE GREATNESS OF THE LORD" (LUKE 1:46)

How can we speak about gratitude and encouragement without looking to Mary? She, the woman whose heart was pierced (cf. Luke 2:35), teaches us the praise capable of lifting our gaze to the future and restoring hope to the present. Her entire life was contained in her song of praise (cf. Luke 1:46–55). We too are called to sing that song as a promise of future fulfilment.

Whenever I visit a Marian shrine, I like to spend time looking at the Blessed Mother and letting her look at me. I pray for a childlike trust, the trust of the poor and simple who know that their mother is there, and that they have a place in her heart. And in looking at her, to hear once more, like the Indian Juan Diego: "My youngest son, what is the matter? Do not let it disturb your heart. Am I not here, I who have the honour to be your mother?"[33]

To contemplate Mary is "to believe once again in the revolutionary nature of love and tenderness. In her, we see that humility and tenderness are not virtues of the weak but of the strong, who need not treat others poorly in order to feel important themselves."[34]

Perhaps at times our gaze can begin to harden, or we can feel that the seductive power of apathy or self-pity is about to take root in our heart. Or our sense of being a living and integral part of God's People begins to weary us, and we feel tempted to a certain elitism. At those times, let us not be afraid to turn to Mary and to take up her song of praise.

Perhaps at times we can feel tempted to withdraw into ourselves and our own affairs, safe from the dusty paths of daily life. Or regrets, complaints, criticism and sarcasm gain the upper hand and make us lose our desire to keep fighting, hoping and loving. At those times, let us look to Mary so that she can free our gaze of all the "clutter" that prevents us from being attentive and alert, and thus capable of seeing and celebrating Christ alive in the midst of his people. And if we see that we are going astray, or that we are failing in our attempts at conversion, then let us turn to her like a great parish priest from my previous diocese, who was also a poet. He asked her, with something of a smile: "This evening, dear Lady / my promise is sincere; / but just to be sure, don't forget / to leave the key outside the door."[35] Our Lady "is the friend who is ever concerned that wine not be lacking in our lives. She is the woman whose heart was pierced by a sword and who understands all our pain. As mother of all, she is a sign of hope for peoples suffering the birth pangs of justice....As a true mother, she walks at our side, she shares our struggles and she constantly surrounds us with God's love."[36]

Dear brothers, once more, "I do not cease to give thanks for you" (Eph 1:16), for your commitment and your ministry. For I am confident that "God takes away even the hardest stones against which our hopes and expectations crash: death, sin, fear, worldliness. Human history does not end before a tombstone, because today it encounters the 'living stone' (cf. 1 Pet 2:4), the risen Jesus. We, as Church, are built on him, and, even when we grow disheartened and tempted to judge everything in the light of our failures, he comes to make all things new."[37]

May we allow our gratitude to awaken praise and renewed enthusiasm for our ministry of anointing our brothers and sisters with hope. May we be men whose lives bear witness to the compassion and mercy that Jesus alone can bestow on us.

May the Lord Jesus bless you and the Holy Virgin watch over you. And please, I ask you not to forget to pray for me.

Notes

1. Cf. Apostolic Letter *Anno Iubilari* (23 April 1929): *AAS* 21 (1929), 312–313.

2. *Address to the Italian Bishops' Conference* (20 May 2019). Spiritual fatherhood requires a bishop not to leave his priests as orphans; it can be felt not only in his readiness to open his doors to priests, but also to seek them out in order to care for them and to accompany them.

3. Cf. Saint John XXIII, Encyclical Letter *Sacerdotii Nostri Primordia (On the Hundredth Anniversary of the Death of the Holy Curé of Ars)* (1 August 1959): *AAS* 51 (1959), 548.

4. Cf. *Letter to the People of God* (20 August 2018).

5. *Meeting with Priests, Religious, Consecrated Persons and Seminarians, Santiago de Chile* (16 January 2018).

6. Cf. *Letter to the Pilgrim People of God in Chile* (31 May 2018).

7. *Meeting with the Priests of the Diocese of Rome* (7 March 2019).

8. *Homily at the Easter Vigil* (19 April 2014).

9. Apostolic Exhortation *Gaudete et Exsultate*, 7.

10. Cf. Jorge Mario Bergoglio, *Las cartas de la tribulación* (Herder, 2019), 21.

11. Cf. *Address to the Parish Priests of Rome* (6 March 2014).

12. *Retreat to Priests. First Meditation* (2 June 2016).

13. A. Spadaro, Interview with Pope Francis, in *La Civiltà Cattolica* 3918 (19 September 2013), p. 462.

14. Apostolic Exhortation *Evangelii Gaudium*, 137.

15. Cf. *Address to the Parish Priests of Rome* (6 March 2014).

16. Cf. Apostolic Exhortation *Evangelii Gaudium*, 268.

17. Apostolic Exhortation *Gaudete et Exsultate*, 7.

18. Cf. Apostolic Letter *Misericordia et Misera*, 13.

19. Apostolic Exhortation *Gaudete et Exsultate*, 50.

20. Ibid., 134.

21. Cf. Jorge Mario Bergoglio, *Reflexiones en esperanza* (Vatican City, 2013), p. 14.

22. *Journal d'un curé de campagne* (Paris, 1974), p. 135; cf. Apostolic Exhortation *Evangelii Gaudium*, 83.

23. Cf. Barsanuph of Gaza, *Letters*, in Vito Cutro—Michal Tadeusz Szwemin, *Bisogno di paternità* (Warsaw, 2018), p. 124.

24. L'arte di purificare il cuore, Rome, 1999, p. 47.

25. Apostolic Exhortation *Evangelii Gaudium*, 2.

26. Apostolic Exhortation *Gaudete et Exsultate*, 137.

27. Apostolic Exhortation *Evangelii Gaudium*, 1.

28. Ibid., 3.

29. Jorge Mario Bergoglio, *Reflexiones en esperanza* (Vatican City, 2013), p. 26.

30. Apostolic Exhortation *Evangelii Gaudium*, 94.

31. *Meeting with Clergy, Consecrated Persons and Members of Pastoral Councils*, Assisi (4 October 2013).

32. Cf. Apostolic Exhortation *Evangelii Gaudium*, 268–270.

33. *Nican Mopohua*, 107, 118, 119.

34. Apostolic Exhortation *Evangelii Gaudium*, 288.

35. Cf. Amelio Luis Calori, *Aula Fúlgida*, Buenos Aires, 1946.

36. Apostolic Exhortation *Evangelii Gaudium*, 286.

37. *Homily at the Easter Vigil* (20 April 2019).

CHAPTER ONE

God's Anointed Ones

*Homily of Pope Francis, Saint Peter's Basilica,
Holy Thursday, March 28, 2013*

Dear Brothers and Sisters,

This morning I have the joy of celebrating my first Chrism Mass as the Bishop of Rome. I greet all of you with affection, especially you, dear priests, who, like myself, today recall the day of your ordination.

The readings and the Psalm of our Mass speak of God's "anointed ones": the suffering Servant of Isaiah, King David and Jesus our Lord. All three have this in common: the anointing that they receive is meant in turn to anoint God's faithful people, whose servants they are; they are anointed for the poor, for prisoners, for the oppressed....A fine image of this "being for" others can be found in Psalm 133: "It is like the precious oil upon the head, running down upon the beard, on the beard of Aaron, running down upon the collar of his robe" (v. 2). The image of spreading oil, flowing down from the beard of Aaron upon the collar of his sacred robe, is an image of the priestly anointing which, through Christ, the Anointed One, reaches the ends of the earth, represented by the robe.

The sacred robes of the High Priest are rich in symbolism. One such symbol is that the names of the children of Israel were engraved on the onyx stones mounted on the shoulder-pieces of the ephod, the ancestor of our present-day chasuble: six on the stone of the right shoulder-piece and six on that of the left (cf. Exod 28:6–14). The names of the twelve tribes of Israel were also engraved on the breastplate (cf. Exod 28:21). This means that the priest celebrates by carrying on his shoulders the people entrusted to his care and bearing their names written in his heart. When we put on our simple chasuble, it might well make us feel, upon our shoulders and in our hearts, the burdens and the faces of our faithful people, our saints and martyrs who are numerous in these times.

From the beauty of all these liturgical things, which is not so much about trappings and fine fabrics than about the glory of our God resplendent in his people, alive and strengthened, we turn now to a consideration of activity, action. The precious oil which anoints the head of Aaron does more than simply lend fragrance to his person; it overflows down to "the edges." The Lord will say this clearly: his anointing is meant for the poor, prisoners and the sick, for those who are sorrowing and alone. My dear brothers, the ointment is not intended just to make us fragrant, much less to be kept in a jar, for then it would become rancid…and the heart bitter.

A good priest can be recognized by the way his people are anointed: this is a clear proof. When our people are anointed with the oil of gladness, it is obvious: for example, when they leave Mass looking as if they have heard good news. Our people like to hear the Gospel preached with "unction," they like it when the Gospel we preach touches their daily lives, when it runs down like the oil of Aaron to the edges of reality, when it brings light to moments of extreme darkness, to the "outskirts" where people of faith are most exposed to the onslaught of those who want to tear down their faith. People thank us because they feel that we have prayed over the realities of their everyday lives, their troubles, their joys, their burdens and their hopes. And when they feel that the fragrance of the Anointed One, of Christ, has come to them through us, they feel encouraged to entrust to us everything they want to bring before the Lord: "Pray for me, Father, because I have this problem," "Bless me Father," "Pray for me"—these words are the sign that the anointing has flowed down to the edges of the robe, for it has turned into a prayer of supplication, the supplication of the People of God. When we have this relationship with God and with his people, and grace passes through us, then we are priests, mediators between God and men. What I want to emphasize is that we need constantly to stir up God's grace and perceive in every request, even those requests that are inconvenient and at times purely material or downright banal—but only apparently so—the desire of our people to be anointed with fragrant oil, since they know that we have it. To perceive and to sense, even as the Lord sensed the hope-filled anguish of the woman suffering from hemorrhages when she touched the hem of his garment. At that moment, Jesus, surrounded by people on every side, embodies all the beauty of Aaron vested in priestly raiment, with the oil running down upon his robes. It is a hidden beauty, one which shines forth only for those faith-filled eyes of the woman troubled with an issue of blood. But not even the disciples—future priests—see or understand: on the "existential outskirts," they see only what is on the surface: the crowd pressing in on Jesus from all sides (cf. Luke 8:42). The Lord, on the other hand, feels the power of the divine anointing which runs down to the edge of his cloak.

We need to "go out," then, in order to experience our own anointing, its power and its redemptive efficacy: to the "outskirts" where there is suffering, bloodshed, blindness that longs for sight, and prisoners in thrall to many evil masters. It is not in soul-searching or constant introspection that we encounter the Lord: self-help courses can be useful in life, but to live our priestly life going from one course to another, from one method to another, leads us to become pelagians and to minimize the power of grace, which comes alive and flourishes to the extent that we, in faith, go out and give ourselves and the Gospel to others, giving what little ointment we have to those who have nothing, nothing at all.

The priest who seldom goes out of himself, who anoints little—I won't say "not at all," because, thank God, the people take the oil from us anyway—misses out on the best of our people, on what can stir the depths of his priestly heart. Those who do not go out of themselves, instead of being mediators, gradually become intermediaries, managers. We know the difference: the intermediary, the manager, "has already received his reward," and since he doesn't put his own skin and his own heart on the line, he never hears a warm, heartfelt word of thanks. This is precisely the reason for the dissatisfaction of some, who end up sad—sad priests—in some sense becoming collectors of antiques or novelties, instead of being shepherds living with "the odour of the sheep." This I ask you: be shepherds, with the "odour of the sheep." Make it real, as shepherds among your flock, fishers of men. True enough, the so-called crisis of priestly identity threatens us all and adds to the broader cultural crisis; but if we can resist its onslaught, we will be able to put out in the name of the Lord and cast our nets. It is not a bad thing that reality itself forces us to "put out into the deep," where what we are by grace is clearly seen as pure grace, out into the deep of the contemporary world, where the only thing that counts is "unction"—not function—and the nets which overflow with fish are those cast solely in the name of the One in whom we have put our trust: Jesus.

Dear lay faithful, be close to your priests with affection and with your prayers, that they may always be shepherds according to God's heart.

Dear priests, may God the Father renew in us the Spirit of holiness with whom we have been anointed. May he renew his Spirit in our hearts, that this anointing may spread to everyone, even to those "outskirts" where our faithful people most look for it and most appreciate it. May our people sense that we are the Lord's disciples; may they feel that their names are written upon our priestly vestments and that we seek no other identity; and may they receive through our words and deeds the oil of gladness which Jesus, the Anointed One, came to bring us. Amen.

CHAPTER TWO

Priestly Joy

Holy Chrism Mass, Homily of Pope Francis, Vatican Basilica,
Holy Thursday, April 17, 2014

In the eternal "today" of Holy Thursday, when Christ showed his love for us to the end (cf. John 13:1), we recall the happy day of the institution of the priesthood, as well as the day of our own priestly ordination. The Lord anointed us in Christ with the oil of gladness, and this anointing invites us to accept and appreciate this great gift: the gladness, the joy of being a priest. Priestly joy is a priceless treasure, not only for the priest himself, but for the entire faithful people of God: that faithful people from which he is called to be anointed and which he, in turn, is sent to anoint.

Anointed with the oil of gladness so as to anoint others with the oil of gladness. Priestly joy has its source in the Father's love, and the Lord wishes the joy of this Love to be "ours" and to be "complete" (John 15:11). I like to reflect on joy by contemplating Our Lady, for Mary, the "Mother of the living Gospel, is a wellspring of joy for God's little ones" (*Evangelii Gaudium* 288). I do not think it is an exaggeration to say that the priest is very little indeed: the incomparable grandeur of the gift granted us for the ministry sets us among the least of men. The priest is the poorest of men unless Jesus enriches him by his poverty, the most useless of servants unless Jesus calls him his friend, the most ignorant of men unless Jesus patiently teaches him as he did Peter, the frailest of Christians unless the Good Shepherd strengthens him in the midst of the flock. No one is more "little" than a priest left to his own devices; and so our prayer of protection against every snare of the Evil One is the prayer of our Mother: I am a priest because he has regarded my littleness (cf. Luke 1:48). And in that littleness we find our joy. Joy in our littleness!

For me, there are three significant features of our priestly joy. It is a joy which *anoints us* (not one which "greases" us, making us unctuous, sumptuous and presumptuous), it is a joy which is *imperishable* and it is a *missionary* joy which spreads and attracts, starting backwards—with those farthest away from us.

A joy which anoints us. In a word: it has penetrated deep within our hearts, it has shaped them and strengthened them sacramentally. The signs of the ordination liturgy speak to us of the Church's maternal desire to pass on and share with others all that the Lord has given us: the laying on of hands, the anointing with sacred chrism, the clothing with sacred vestments, the first consecration which immediately follows…. Grace fills us to the brim and overflows, fully, abundantly and entirely in each priest. We are anointed down to our very bones…and our joy, which wells up from deep within, is the echo of this anointing.

An imperishable joy. The fullness of the Gift, which no one can take away or increase, is an unfailing source of joy: an imperishable joy which the Lord has promised no one can take from us (John 16:22). It can lie dormant, or be clogged by sin or by life's troubles, yet deep down it remains intact, like the embers of a burnt log beneath the ashes, and it can always be renewed. Paul's exhortation to Timothy remains ever timely: I remind you to fan into flame the gift of God that is within you through the laying on of my hands (cf. 2 Tim 1:6).

A missionary joy. I would like especially to share with you and to stress this third feature: priestly joy is deeply bound up with God's holy and faithful people, for it is an eminently missionary joy. Our anointing is meant for anointing God's holy and faithful people: for baptizing and confirming them, healing and sanctifying them, blessing, comforting and evangelizing them.

And since this joy is one which only springs up when the shepherd is in the midst of his flock (for even in the silence of his prayer, the shepherd who worships the Father is with his sheep), it is a "guarded joy," watched over by the flock itself. Even in those gloomy moments when everything looks dark and a feeling of isolation takes hold of us, in those moments of listlessness and boredom which at times overcome us in our priestly life (and which I too have experienced), even in those moments God's people are able to "guard" that joy; they are able to protect you, to embrace you and to help you open your heart to find renewed joy.

A "guarded joy": one guarded by the flock but also guarded by three sisters who surround it, tend it and defend it: sister poverty, sister fidelity, and sister obedience.

The joy of priests is a joy which is sister to poverty. The priest is poor in terms of purely human joy. He has given up so much! And because he is poor, he, who gives so much to others, has to seek his joy from the Lord and from God's faithful people. He doesn't need to try to create it for himself. We know that our people are very generous in thanking priests for their slightest blessing and especially for the sacraments. Many people, in speaking of the crisis of priestly identity, fail to realize that identity presupposes belonging. There is no identity—and consequently joy of life—without an active and unwavering sense of belonging to God's faithful people (cf. *Evangelii Gaudium* 268). The priest who tries to find his priestly identity by soul-searching and introspection may well encounter nothing more than "exit" signs, signs that say: exit from yourself, exit to seek God in adoration, go out and give your people what was entrusted to you, for your people will make you feel and taste who you are, what your name is, what your identity is, and they will make you rejoice in that hundredfold which the Lord has promised to those who serve him. Unless you "exit" from yourself, the oil grows rancid and the anointing cannot be fruitful. Going out from ourselves presupposes self-denial; it means poverty.

Priestly joy is a joy which is sister to fidelity. Not primarily in the sense that we are all "immaculate" (would that by God's grace we were!), for we are sinners, but in the sense of an ever renewed fidelity to the one Bride, to the Church. Here fruitfulness is key. The spiritual children which the Lord gives each priest, the children he has baptized, the families he has blessed and helped on their way, the sick he has comforted, the young people he catechizes and helps to grow, the poor he assists…all these are the "Bride" whom he rejoices to treat as his supreme and only love and to whom he is constantly faithful. It is the living Church, with a first name and a last name, which the priest shepherds in his parish or in the mission entrusted to him. That mission brings him joy whenever he is faithful to it, whenever he does all that he has to do and lets go of everything that he has to let go of, as long as he stands firm amid the flock which the Lord has entrusted to him: Feed my sheep (cf. John 21:16, 17).

Priestly joy is a joy which is sister to obedience. An obedience to the Church in the hierarchy which gives us, as it were, not simply the external framework for our obedience: the parish to which I am sent, my ministerial assignments, my particular work...but also union with God the Father, the source of all fatherhood. It is likewise an obedience to the Church in service: in availability and readiness to serve everyone, always and as best I can, following the example of "Our Lady of Promptness" (cf. Luke 1:39, [in Greek] *meta spoudes*), who hastens to serve Elizabeth her kinswoman and is concerned for the kitchen of Cana when the wine runs out. The availability of her priests makes the Church a house with open doors, a refuge for sinners, a home for people living on the streets, a place of loving care for the sick, a camp for the young, a classroom for catechizing children about to make their First Communion....Wherever God's people have desires or needs, there is the priest, who knows how to listen ([in Latin] *ob-audire*) and feels a loving mandate from Christ who sends him to relieve that need with mercy or to encourage those good desires with resourceful charity.

All who are called should know that genuine and complete joy does exist in this world: it is the joy of being taken from the people we love and then being sent back to them as dispensers of the gifts and counsels of Jesus, the one Good Shepherd who, with deep compassion for all the little ones and the outcasts of this earth, wearied and oppressed like sheep without a shepherd, wants to associate many others to his ministry, so as himself to remain with us and to work, in the person of his priests, for the good of his people.

On this Holy Thursday, I ask the Lord Jesus to enable many young people to discover that burning zeal which joy kindles in our hearts as soon as we have the stroke of boldness needed to respond willingly to his call.

On this Holy Thursday, I ask the Lord Jesus to preserve the joy sparkling in the eyes of the recently ordained who go forth to devour the world, to spend themselves fully in the midst of God's faithful people, rejoicing as they prepare their first homily, their first Mass, their first Baptism, their first confession....It is the joy of being able to share with wonder, and for the first time as God's anointed, the treasure of the Gospel and to feel the faithful people anointing you again and in yet another way: by their requests, by bowing their heads for your blessing, by taking your hands, by bringing you their children, by pleading for their sick....Preserve, Lord, in your young priests the joy of going forth, of doing everything as if for the first time, the joy of spending their lives fully for you.

On this Thursday of the priesthood, I ask the Lord Jesus to confirm the priestly joy of those who have already ministered for some years. The joy which, without leaving their eyes, is also found on the shoulders of those who bear the burden of the ministry, those priests who, having experienced the labours of the apostolate, gather their strength and rearm themselves: "get a second wind," as the athletes say. Lord, preserve the depth, wisdom and maturity of the joy felt by these older priests. May they be able to pray with Nehemiah: "the joy of the Lord is my strength" (cf. Neh 8:10).

Finally, on this Thursday of the priesthood, I ask the Lord Jesus to make better known the joy of elderly priests, whether healthy or infirm. It is the joy of the Cross, which springs from the knowledge that we possess an imperishable treasure in perishable earthen vessels. May these priests find happiness wherever they are; may they experience already, in the passage of the years, a taste of eternity (Guardini). May they know, Lord, the joy of handing on the torch, the joy of seeing new generations of their spiritual children, and of hailing the promises from afar, smiling and at peace, in that hope which does not disappoint.

CHAPTER THREE

Witnesses and Ministers of the Father's Mercy

Holy Chrism Mass, Homily of His Holiness Pope Francis,
Vatican Basilica, Holy Thursday, March 24, 2016

After hearing Jesus read from the Prophet Isaiah and say: "Today this Scripture has been fulfilled in your hearing" (Luke 4:21), the congregation in the synagogue of Nazareth might well have burst into applause. They might have then wept for joy, as did the people when Nehemiah and Ezra the priest read from the book of the Law found while they were rebuilding the walls. But the Gospels tell us that Jesus' townspeople did the opposite; they closed their hearts to him and sent him off. At first, "all spoke well of him, and wondered at the gracious words that came from his mouth" (4:22). But then an insidious question began to make the rounds: "Is this not the son of Joseph, the carpenter?" (4:22). And then, "they were filled with rage" (4:28). They wanted to throw him off the cliff. This was in fulfilment of the elderly Simeon's prophecy to the Virgin Mary that he would be "a sign of contradiction" (2:34). By his words and actions, Jesus lays bare the secrets of the heart of every man and woman.

Where the Lord proclaims the Gospel of the Father's unconditional mercy to the poor, the outcast and the oppressed, is the very place we are called to take a stand, to "fight the good fight of the faith" (1 Tim 6:12). His battle is not against men and women, but against the devil (cf. Eph 6:12), the enemy of humanity. But the Lord "passes through the midst" of all those who would stop him and "continues on his way" (Luke 4:30). Jesus does not fight to build power. If he breaks down walls and challenges our sense of security, he does this to open the flood gates of that mercy which, with the Father and the Holy Spirit, he wants to pour out upon our world. A mercy which expands; it proclaims and brings newness; it heals, liberates and proclaims the year of the Lord's favour.

The mercy of our God is infinite and indescribable. We express the power of this mystery as an "ever greater" mercy, a mercy in motion, a mercy that each day seeks to make progress, taking small steps forward and advancing in that wasteland where indifference and violence have predominated.

This was the way of the Good Samaritan, who "showed mercy" (cf. Luke 10:37): he was moved, he drew near to the wounded man, he bandaged his wounds, took him to the inn, stayed there that evening and promised to return and cover any further cost. This is the way of mercy, which gathers together small gestures. Without demeaning, it grows with each helpful sign and act of love. Every one of us, looking at our own lives as God does, can try to remember the ways in which the Lord has been merciful towards us, how he has been much more merciful than we imagined. In this we can find the courage to ask him to take a step further and to reveal yet more of his mercy in the future: "Show us, Lord, your mercy" (Ps 85:8). This paradoxical way of praying to an ever more merciful God, helps us to tear down those walls with which we try to contain the abundant greatness of his heart. It is good for us to break out of our set ways, because it is proper to the Heart of God to overflow with tenderness, with ever more to give. For the Lord prefers something to be wasted rather than one drop of mercy be held back. He would rather have many seeds be carried off by the birds of the air than have one seed be missing, since each of those seeds has the capacity to bear abundant fruit, thirtyfold, sixtyfold, even a hundredfold.

As priests, we are witnesses to and ministers of the ever-increasing abundance of the Father's mercy; we have the rewarding and consoling task of incarnating mercy, as Jesus did, who "went about doing good and healing" (Acts 10:38) in a thousand ways so that it could touch everyone. We can help to inculturate mercy, so that each person can embrace it and experience it personally. This will help all people truly understand and practise mercy with creativity, in ways that respect their local cultures and families.

Today, during this Holy Thursday of the Jubilee Year of Mercy, I would like to speak of two areas in which the Lord shows excess in mercy. Based on his example, we also should not hesitate in showing excess. The first area I am referring to is encounter; the second is God's forgiveness, which shames us while also giving us dignity.

The first area where we see *God showing excess* in his ever-increasing mercy is that of *encounter*. He gives himself completely and in such a way that every encounter leads to rejoicing. In the parable of the Merciful Father we are astounded by the man who runs, deeply moved, to his son, and throws his arms around him; we see how he embraces his son, kisses him, puts a ring on his finger, and then gives him his sandals, thus show-ing that he is a son and not a servant. Finally, he gives orders to everyone and organizes a party. In contemplating with awe this superabundance of the Father's joy that is freely and bound-lessly expressed when his son returns, we should not be fearful of exaggerating our gratitude. Our attitude should be that of the poor leper who, seeing himself healed, leaves his nine friends who go off to do what Jesus ordered, and goes back to kneel at the feet of the Lord, glorifying and thanking God aloud.

Mercy restores everything; it restores dignity to each person. This is why effusive gratitude is the proper response: we have to go to the party, to put on our best clothes, to cast off the rancour of the elder brother, to rejoice and give thanks....Only in this way, participating fully in such rejoicing, is it possible to think straight, to ask for forgiveness, and see more clearly how to make up for the evil we have committed. It would be good for us to ask ourselves: after going to con-fession, do I rejoice? Or do I move on immediately to the next thing, as we would after going to the doctor, when we hear that the test results are not so bad and put them back in their envelope? And when I give alms, do I give time to the person who receives them to express their gratitude, do I celebrate the smile and the blessings that the poor offer, or do I continue on in haste with my own affairs after tossing in a coin?

The second area in which we see how *God exceeds* in his ever greater mercy is *forgiveness itself*. God does not only forgive incalculable debts, as he does to that servant who begs for mercy but is then miserly to his own debtor; he also enables us to move directly from the most shameful disgrace to the highest dignity without any intermediary stages. The Lord allows the forgiven woman to wash his feet with her tears. As soon as Simon con-fesses his sin and begs Jesus to send him away, the Lord raises him to be a fisher of men. We, however, tend to separate these two attitudes: when we are ashamed of our sins, we hide ourselves and walk around with our heads down, like Adam and Eve; and when we are raised up to some dignity, we try to cover up our sins and take pleasure in being seen, almost showing off.

Our response to God's superabundant forgiveness should be always to preserve *that healthy tension between a dignified shame and a shamed dignity*. It is the attitude of one who seeks a humble and lowly place, but who can also allow the Lord to raise him up for the good of the mission, without complacency. The model that the Gospel consecrates, and which can help us when we confess our sins, is Peter, who allowed himself to be questioned about his love for the Lord, but who also renewed his acceptance of the ministry of shepherding the flock which the Lord had entrusted to him.

To grow in this "dignity which is capable of humbling itself," and which delivers us from thinking that we are more or are less than what we are by grace, can help us understand the words of the Prophet Isaiah that immediately follow the passage our Lord read in the synagogue at Nazareth: "You will be called priests of the Lord, ministers of our God" (Isa 61:6). It is people who are poor, hungry, prisoners of war, without a future, cast to one side and rejected, that the Lord transforms into a priestly people.

As priests, we identify with people who are excluded, people the Lord saves. We remind ourselves that there are countless masses of people who are poor, uneducated, prisoners, who find themselves in such situations because others oppress them. But we too remember that each of us knows the extent to which we too are often blind, lacking the radiant light of faith, not because we do not have the Gospel close at hand, but because of an excess of complicated theology. We feel that our soul thirsts for spirituality, not for a lack of Living Water which we only sip from, but because of an excessive "bubbly" spirituality, a "light" spirituality. We feel ourselves also trapped, not so much by insurmountable stone walls or steel enclosures that affect many peoples, but rather by a digital, virtual worldliness that is opened and closed by a simple *click*. We are oppressed, not by threats and pressures, like so many poor people, but by the allure of a thousand commercial advertisements which we cannot shrug off to walk ahead, freely, along paths that lead us to love of our brothers and sisters, to the Lord's flock, to the sheep who wait for the voice of their shepherds.

Jesus comes to redeem us, to send us out, to transform us from being poor and blind, imprisoned and oppressed, to become ministers of mercy and consolation. He says to us, using the words the prophet Ezekiel spoke to the people who sold themselves and betrayed the Lord: "I will remember my covenant with you in the days of your youth….Then you will remember your ways, and be ashamed when I take your sisters, both your elder and your younger, and give them to you as daughters, but not on account of the covenant with you. I will establish my covenant with you, and you shall know that I am the Lord, that you may remember and be confounded, and never open your mouth again because of your shame, when I forgive you all that you have done, says the Lord God" (Ezek 16:60–63).

In this Jubilee Year we celebrate our Father with hearts full of gratitude, and we pray to him that "he remember his mercy forever"; let us receive, with a dignity that is able to humble itself, the mercy revealed in the wounded flesh of our Lord Jesus Christ. Let us ask him to cleanse us of all sin and free us from every evil. And with the grace of the Holy Spirit let us commit ourselves anew to bringing God's mercy to all men and women, and performing those works which the Spirit inspires in each of us for the common good of the entire People of God.

CHAPTER FOUR

Spending Time
with Jesus

Holy Chrism Mass, Homily of His Holiness Pope Francis,
Vatican Basilica, Holy Thursday, April 2, 2015

"My hand shall ever abide with him, my arms also shall strengthen him" (Ps 89:21).

This is what the Lord means when he says: "I have found David, my servant; with my holy oil I have anointed him" (v. 20). It is also what our Father thinks whenever he "encounters" a priest. And he goes on to say: "My faithfulness and my steadfast love shall be with him....He shall cry to me, 'You are my Father, my God and the rock of my salvation'" (vv. 24, 26).

It is good to enter with the Psalmist into this monologue of our God. He is talking about us, his priests, his pastors. But it is not really a monologue since he is not the only one speaking. The Father says to Jesus: "Your friends, those who love you, can say to me in a particular way: 'You are my Father'" (cf. John 14:21). If the Lord is so concerned about helping us, it is because he knows that the task of anointing his faithful people is not easy, it is demanding; it can tire us. We experience this in so many ways: from the ordinary fatigue brought on by our daily apostolate to the weariness of sickness, death and even martyrdom.

The tiredness of priests! Do you know how often I think about this weariness which all of you experience? I think about it and I pray about it, often, especially when I am tired myself. I pray for you as you labour amid the people of God entrusted to your care, many of you in lonely and dangerous places. Our weariness, dear priests, is like incense, which silently rises up to heaven (cf. Ps 141:2; Rev 8:3–4). Our weariness goes straight to the heart of the Father.

Know that the Blessed Virgin Mary is well aware of this tiredness and she brings it straight to the Lord. As our Mother, she knows when her children are weary, and this is her greatest concern. "Welcome! Rest, my child. We will speak afterwards…." Whenever we draw near to her, she says to us: "Am I not here with you, I who am your Mother?" (cf. *Evangelii Gaudium* 286). And to her Son she will say, as she did at Cana, "They have no wine" (John 2:3).

It can also happen that, whenever we feel weighed down by pastoral work, we can be tempted to rest however we please, as if rest were not itself a gift of God. We must not fall into this temptation. Our weariness is precious in the eyes of Jesus who embraces us and lifts us up. "Come to me, all who labour and are overburdened, and I will give you rest" (Matt 11:28). Whenever a priest feels dead tired, yet is able to bow down in adoration and say: "Enough for today Lord," and entrust himself to the Father, he knows that he will not fall but be renewed. The one who anoints God's faithful people with oil is also himself anointed by the Lord: "He gives you a garland instead of ashes, the oil of gladness instead of mourning, the mantle of praise instead of a faint spirit" (cf. Isa 61:3).

Let us never forget that a key to fruitful priestly ministry lies in how we rest and in how we look at the way the Lord deals with our weariness. How difficult it is to learn how to rest! This says much about our trust and our ability to realize that that we too are sheep: we need the help of the Shepherd. A few questions can help us in this regard.

Do I know how to rest by accepting the love, gratitude and affection which I receive from God's faithful people? Or, once my pastoral work is done, do I seek more refined relaxations, not those of the poor but those provided by a consumerist society? Is the Holy Spirit truly "rest in times of weariness" for me, or is he just someone who keeps me busy? Do I know how to seek help from a wise priest? Do I know how to take a break from myself, from the demands I make on myself, from my self-seeking and from my self-absorption? Do I know how to spend time with Jesus, with the Father, with the Virgin Mary and Saint Joseph, with my patron saints, and to find rest in their demands, which are easy and light, and in their pleasures, for they delight to be in my company, and in their concerns and standards, which have only to do with the greater glory of God? Do I know how to rest from my enemies under the Lord's protection? Am I preoccupied with how I should speak and act, or do I entrust myself to the Holy Spirit, who will teach me what I need to say in every situation? Do I worry needlessly, or, like Paul, do I find repose by saying: "I know him in whom I have placed my trust" (2 Tim 1:12)?

Let us return for a moment to what today's liturgy describes as the work of the priest: to bring good news to the poor, to proclaim freedom to prisoners and healing to the blind, to offer liberation to the downtrodden and to announce the year of the Lord's favour. Isaiah also mentions consoling the broken-hearted and comforting the afflicted.

These are not easy or purely mechanical jobs, like running an office, building a parish hall or laying out a soccer field for the young of the parish....The tasks of which Jesus speaks call for the ability to show compassion; our hearts are to be "moved" and fully engaged in carrying them out. We are to rejoice with couples who marry; we are to laugh with the children brought to the baptismal font; we are to accompany young fiancés and families; we are to suffer with those who receive the anointing of the sick in their hospital beds; we are to mourn with those burying a loved one....All these emotions...if we do not have an open heart, can exhaust the heart of a shepherd. For us priests, what happens in the lives of our people is not like a news bulletin: we know our people, we sense what is going on in their hearts. Our own heart, sharing in their suffering, feels "com-passion," is exhausted, broken into a thousand pieces, moved and even "consumed" by the people. Take this, eat this...These are the words the priest of Jesus whispers repeatedly while caring for his faithful people: Take this, eat this; take this, drink this....In this way our priestly life is given over in service, in closeness to the People of God...and this always leaves us weary.

I wish to share with you some forms of weariness on which I have meditated.

There is what we can call "the weariness of people, the weariness of the crowd." For the Lord, and for us, this can be exhausting—so the Gospel tells us—yet it is a good weariness, a fruitful and joyful exhaustion. The people who followed Jesus, the families which brought their children to him to be blessed, those who had been cured, those who came with their friends, the young people who were so excited about the Master...they did not even leave him time to eat. But the Lord never tired of being with people. On the contrary, he seemed renewed by their presence (cf. *Evangelii Gaudium* 11). This weariness in the midst of activity is a grace on which all priests can draw (cf. *Ibid.*, 279). And how beautiful it is! People love their priests, they want and need their shepherds! The faithful never leave us without something to do, unless we hide in our offices or go out in our cars wearing sun glasses. There is a good and healthy tiredness. It is the exhaustion of the priest who wears the smell of the sheep...but also smiles the smile of a father rejoicing in his children or grandchildren. It has nothing to do with those who wear expensive cologne and who look at others from afar and from above (cf. *Ibid.*, 97). We are the friends of the Bridegroom: this is our joy. If Jesus is shepherding the flock in our midst, we cannot be shepherds who are glum, plaintive or, even worse, bored. The smell of the sheep and the smile of a father....Weary, yes, but with the joy of those who hear the Lord saying: "Come, O blessed of my Father" (Matt 25:34).

There is also the kind of weariness which we can call "the weariness of enemies." The Devil and his minions never sleep and, since their ears cannot bear to hear the word of God, they work tirelessly to silence that word and to distort it. Confronting them is more wearying. It involves not only doing good, with all the exertion this entails, but also defending the flock and oneself from evil (cf. *Evangelii Gaudium* 83). The evil one is far more astute than we are, and he is able to demolish in a moment what it took us years of patience to build up. Here we need to implore the grace to learn how to "offset" (and it is an important habit to acquire): to thwart evil without pulling up the good wheat, or presuming to protect like supermen what the Lord alone can protect. All this helps us not to let our guard down before the depths of iniquity, before the mockery of the wicked. In these situations of weariness, the Lord says to us: "Have courage! I have overcome the world!" (John 16:33). The word of God gives us strength.

And finally—I say finally lest you be too wearied by this homily itself!—there is also "weariness of ourselves" (cf. *Evangelii Gaudium* 277). This may be the most dangerous weariness of all. That is because the other two kinds come from being exposed, from going out of ourselves to anoint and to do battle (for our job is to care for others). But this third kind of weariness is more "self-referential." It is dissatisfaction with oneself, but not the dissatisfaction of someone who directly confronts himself and serenely acknowledges his sinfulness and his need for God's mercy, his help; such people ask for help and then move forward. Here we are speaking of a weariness associated with "wanting yet not wanting," having given up everything but continuing to yearn for the fleshpots of Egypt, toying with the illusion of being something different. I like to call this kind of weariness "flirting with spiritual worldliness." When we are alone, we realize how many areas of our life are steeped in this worldliness, so much so that we may feel that it can never be completely washed away. This can be a dangerous kind of weariness. The Book of Revelation shows us the reason for this weariness: "You have borne up for my sake and you have not grown weary. But I have this against you, that you have abandoned the love you had at first" (Rev 2:3–4). Only love gives true rest. What is not loved becomes tiresome, and in time, brings about a harmful weariness.

The most profound and mysterious image of how the Lord deals with our pastoral tiredness is that, "having loved his own, he loved them to the end" (John 13:1): the scene of his washing the feet of his disciples. I like to think of this as the *cleansing of discipleship*. The Lord purifies the path of discipleship itself. He "gets involved" with us (*Evangelii Gaudium* 24), becomes personally responsible for removing every stain, all that grimy, worldly smog which clings to us from the journey we make in his name.

From our feet, we can tell how the rest of our body is doing. The way we follow the Lord reveals how our heart is faring. The wounds on our feet, our sprains and our weariness, are signs of how we have followed him, of the paths we have taken in seeking the lost sheep and in leading the flock to green pastures and still waters (cf. *Ibid.*, 270). The Lord washes us and cleanses us of all the dirt our feet have accumulated in following him. This is something holy. Do not let your feet remain dirty. Like battle wounds, the Lord kisses them and washes away the grime of our labours.

Our discipleship itself is cleansed by Jesus, so that we can rightly feel "joyful," "fulfilled," "free of fear and guilt," and impelled to go out "even to the ends of the earth, to every periphery." In this way we can bring the good news to the most abandoned, knowing that "he is with us always, even to the end of the world." And please, let us ask for the grace to learn how to be weary, but weary in the best of ways!

CHAPTER FIVE

Anointed with the Oil of Mission

Holy Chrism Mass, Homily of His Holiness Pope Francis,
Vatican Basilica, Holy Thursday, April 13, 2017

"The Spirit of the Lord is upon me, because he has anointed me to preach good news to the poor. He has sent me to proclaim release to the captives and recovering of sight to the blind, to set at liberty those who are oppressed" (Luke 4:18). Jesus, anointed by the Spirit, brings *good news* to the poor. Everything he proclaims, and we priests too proclaim, is *good news*. News full of the joy of the Gospel—the joy of those anointed in their sins with the oil of forgiveness and anointed in their charism with the oil of mission, in order to anoint others in turn.

Like Jesus, the priest makes the message joyful with his entire person. When he preaches—briefly, if possible!—he does so with the joy that touches people's hearts with that same word with which the Lord has touched his own heart in prayer. Like every other missionary disciple, the priest makes the message joyful by his whole being. For as we all know, it is in the little things that joy is best seen and shared: when by taking one small step, we make God's mercy overflow in situations of desolation; when we decide to pick up the phone and arrange to see someone; when we patiently allow others to take up our time....

The phrase "*good news*" might appear as just another way of saying "the Gospel." Yet those words point to something essential: the joy of the Gospel. The Gospel is good news because it is, in essence, a message of joy.

The *good news* is the precious pearl of which we read in the Gospel. It is not a thing but a mission. This is evident to anyone who has experienced the "delightful and comforting joy of evangelizing" (*Evangelii Gaudium* 10).

The *good news* is born of Anointing. Jesus' first "great priestly anointing" took place, by the power of the Holy Spirit, in the womb of Mary. The good news of the Annunciation inspired the Virgin Mother to sing her *Magnificat*. It filled the heart of Joseph, her spouse, with sacred silence, and it made John leap for joy in the womb of Elizabeth, his mother.

In today's Gospel, Jesus returns to Nazareth and the joy of the Spirit renews that Anointing in the little synagogue of that town: the Spirit descends and is poured out upon him, "anointing him with the oil of gladness" (cf. Ps 45:8).

Good news. A single word—*Gospel*—that, even as it is spoken, becomes truth, brimming with joy and mercy. We should never attempt to separate these three graces of the Gospel: its truth, which is non-negotiable; its mercy, which is unconditional and offered to all sinners; and its joy, which is personal and open to everyone. Truth, mercy and joy: these three go together.

The truth of the *good news* can never be merely abstract, incapable of taking concrete shape in people's lives because they feel more comfortable seeing it printed in books.

The mercy of the *good news* can never be a false commiseration, one that leaves sinners in their misery without holding out a hand to lift them up and help them take a step in the direction of change.

This message can never be gloomy or indifferent, for it expresses a joy that is completely personal. It is "the joy of the Father, who desires that none of his little ones be lost" (*Evangelii Gaudium* 237). It is the joy of Jesus, who sees that the poor have the good news preached to them, and that the little ones go out to preach the message in turn (*Ibid.*, 5).

The joys of the Gospel are special joys. I say "joys" in the plural, for they are many and varied, depending on how the Spirit chooses to communicate them, in every age, to every person and in every culture. They need to be poured into new wineskins, the ones the Lord speaks of in expressing the newness of his message. I would like to share with you, dear priests, dear brothers, three images or icons of those new wineskins in which the *good news* is kept fresh—for we have to keep it fresh—never turning sour but rather pouring forth in abundance.

A first icon of the *good news* would be the stone water jars at the wedding feast of Cana (cf. John 2:6). In one way, they clearly reflect that perfect vessel which is Our Lady herself, the Virgin Mary. The Gospel tells us that the servants "filled them up to the brim" (John 2:7). I can imagine one of those servants looking to Mary to see if that was enough, and Mary signaling to add one more pailful. Mary is the new wineskin brimming with contagious joy. Without her, dear priests, we cannot move forward in our priesthood! She is "the handmaid of the Father who sings his praises" (*Evangelii Gaudium* 286). Our

Lady of Prompt Succour, who, after conceiving in her immaculate womb the Word of life, goes out to visit and assist her cousin Elizabeth. Her "contagious fullness" helps us overcome the temptation of fear, the temptation to keep ourselves from being filled to the brim and even overflowing, the temptation to a faint-heartedness that holds us back from going forth to fill others with joy. This cannot be, for "the joy of the Gospel fills the hearts and lives of all who encounter Jesus" (*Ibid.*, 1).

A second icon of the *good news* that I would like to share with you today is the jug with its wooden ladle that the Samaritan woman carried on her head in the midday sun (cf. John 4:5–30). It speaks to us of something crucial: the importance of concrete situations. The Lord, the Source of Living Water, had no means of drawing the water to quench his thirst. So the Samaritan woman drew the water with her jug, and with her ladle she sated the Lord's thirst. She sated it even more by concretely confessing her sins. By mercifully shaking the vessel of that Samaritan woman's soul, the Holy Spirit overflowed upon all the people of that small town who asked the Lord to stay with them.

The Lord gave us another new vessel or wineskin full of this "inclusive concreteness" in that Samaritan soul who was Mother Teresa. He called to her and told her: "I am thirsty." He said: "My child, come, take me to the hovels of the poor. Come, be my light. I cannot do this alone. They do not know me, and that is why they do not love me. Bring me to them." Mother Teresa, starting with one concrete person, thanks to her smile and her way of touching their wounds, brought the *good news* to all. The way we touch wounds with our hands, our priestly way of caressing the sick and those who have lost hope. The priest must be a man of tender love. Concreteness and tenderness!

The third icon of the *good news* is the fathomless vessel of the Lord's pierced Heart: his utter meekness, humility and poverty which draw all people to himself. From him we have to learn that announcing a great joy to the poor can only be done in a respectful, humble, and even humbling, way. Concrete, tender and humble: in this way our evangelization will be joyful. Evangelization cannot be presumptuous, nor can the integrity of the truth be rigid, because truth became flesh, it became tenderness, it became a child, it became a man and, on the cross, it became sin (cf. 2 Cor 5:21). The Spirit proclaims and teaches "the whole truth" (cf. John 16:3), and he is not afraid to do this one sip at a time. The Spirit tells us in every situation what we need to say to our enemies (cf. Matt 10:19), and at those times he illumines our every small step forward. This meekness and integrity gives joy to the poor, revives sinners, and grants relief to those oppressed by the devil.

Dear priests, as we contemplate and drink from these three new wineskins, may the *good news* find in us that "contagious fullness" which Our Lady radiates with her whole being, the "inclusive concreteness" of the story of the Samaritan woman, and the "utter meekness" whereby the Holy Spirit ceaselessly wells up and flows forth from the pierced heart of Jesus our Lord.

CHAPTER SIX

Anointed to Anoint

Holy Chrism Mass, Homily of His Holiness Pope Francis,
Vatican Basilica, Holy Thursday, April 18, 2019

The Gospel of Luke, which we just heard, makes us relive the excitement of that moment when the Lord made his own the prophecy of Isaiah, as he read it solemnly in the midst of his people. The synagogue in Nazareth was filled with his relatives, neighbors, acquaintances, friends...and not only. All had their eyes fixed on him. The Church always has her eyes fixed on Jesus Christ, the Anointed One, whom the Spirit sends to anoint God's people.

The Gospels frequently present us with this image of the Lord in the midst of a crowd, surrounded and pressed by people who approach him with their sick ones, who ask him to cast out evil spirits, who hear his teachings and accompany him on the way. "My sheep hear my voice. I know them and they follow me" (John 10:27–28).

The Lord never lost that direct contact with people. Amid those crowds, he always kept the grace of closeness with the people as a whole, and with each individual. We see this throughout his public life, and so it was from the beginning: the radiance of the Child gently attracted shepherds, kings and elderly dreamers like Simeon and Anna. So it was on the cross: his Heart draws all people to himself (John 12:32): Veronicas, Cyreneans, thieves, centurions…

The term "crowd" is not disparaging. Perhaps to some people's ears, it can evoke a faceless, nameless throng….But in the Gospel we see that when the crowd interacts with the Lord—who stands in their midst like a shepherd among his flock—something happens. Deep within, people feel the desire to *follow* Jesus, *amazement* wells up, *discernment* grows apace.

I would like to reflect with you on these three graces that characterize the relationship between Jesus and the crowd.

THE GRACE OF FOLLOWING

Saint Luke says that the crowds "looked for Jesus" (4:42) and "travelled with him" (14:25). They "pressed in on him" and "surrounded him" (8:42–45); they "gathered to hear him" (5:15). Their "following" is something completely unexpected, unconditional and full of affection. It contrasts with the small-mindedness of the disciples, whose attitude towards people verges on cruelty when they suggest to the Lord that he send them away, so that they can get something to eat. Here, I believe, was the beginning of clericalism: in this desire to be assured of a meal and personal comfort without any concern for the people. The Lord cut short that temptation: "You, give them something to eat!" was Jesus' response. "Take care of the people!"

THE GRACE OF AMAZEMENT

The second grace that the crowd receives when it follows Jesus is that of joy-filled amazement. People were amazed by Jesus (Luke 11:14), by his miracles, but above all by his very person. People loved to meet him along the way, to receive his blessing and to bless him, like the woman in the midst of the crowd who blessed his Mother. The Lord himself was amazed by people's faith; he rejoiced and he lost no opportunity to speak about it.

THE GRACE OF DISCERNMENT

The third grace that people receive is that of discernment: "The crowds found out [where Jesus had gone], and followed him" (Luke 9:11). They "were astounded by his teaching, for he taught them as one having authority" (Matt 7:28–29; cf. Luke 5:26). Christ, the Word of God come in the flesh, awakens in people this charism of discernment, which is certainly not the discernment of those who specialize in disputed questions. When the Pharisees and the teachers of the Law debated with him, what people discerned was Jesus' authority, the power of his teaching to touch their hearts, and the fact that evil spirits obeyed him (leaving momentarily speechless those who tried to trap him by their questions; the people liked that; they were able to distinguish this and they liked it).

Let us take a closer look at the way the Gospel views the crowd. Luke points out four large groups who are the preferred beneficiaries of the Lord's anointing: the poor, the blind, the oppressed and captives. He speaks of them in general terms, but then we are glad to see that, in the course of the Lord's life, these anointed ones gradually take on real names and faces. When oil is applied to one part of the body, its beneficial effect is felt throughout the entire body. So too, the Lord, taking up the prophecy of Isaiah, names various "crowds" to whom the Spirit sends him, according to what we may call an "inclusive preferentiality": the grace and the charism given to one individual person or a particular group then redounds, like every action of the Spirit, to the good of all.

The poor (in Greek, *ptochoi*) are those who are bent over, like beggars who bow down and ask for alms. But poor too (*ptochè*) was that widow who anointed with her fingers the two small coins which were all she had to live on that day. *The anointing by the widow to give alms* went unnoticed by the eyes of all except Jesus, who looks kindly on her lowliness. Through her, the Lord can accomplish fully his mission of proclaiming the Gospel to the poor. Paradoxically, the disciples heard the good news that people like her exist. She—the generous woman—could not imagine that she would "make it to the Gospel," that her simple gesture would be recorded in the Gospel. Like all those men and women who are the "saints next door," she lives interiorly the joyful fact that her actions "carry weight" in the Kingdom, and are worth more than all the riches of the world.

The blind are represented by one of the most likable figures in the Gospel: Bartimaeus (cf. Matt 10:46–52), the blind beggar who regained his sight and, from that moment on, only had eyes to follow Jesus on his journey. *The anointing of the gaze!* Our gaze, to which the eyes of Jesus can restore the brightness which only gratuitous love can give, the brightness daily stolen from us by the manipulative and banal images with which the world overwhelms us.

To refer to *the oppressed* (in Greek, *tethrausmenoi*), Luke uses a word that contains the idea of "trauma." It is enough to evoke the parable—perhaps Luke's favourite—of the Good Samaritan, who anoints with oil and binds the wounds (*traumata*: Luke 10:34) of the man who had been beaten by robbers and left lying at the side of the road. *The anointing of the wounded flesh of Christ!* In that anointing we find the remedy for all those traumas that leave individuals, families and entire peoples ignored, excluded and unwanted, on the sidelines of history.

The captives are prisoners of war (in Greek, *aichmalotoi*), those who had been led at the point of a spear (*aichmé*). Jesus would use the same word in speaking of the taking of Jerusalem, his beloved city, and the deportation of its people (Luke 21:24). Our cities today are taken prisoner not so much at spear point, but by more subtle means of ideological colonization.

Only *the anointing of culture*, built up by the labor and the art of our forebears, can free our cities from these new forms of slavery.

As for us, dear brother priests, we must not forget that our evangelical models are those "people," the "crowd" with its real faces, which the anointing of the Lord raises up and revives. They are the ones who complete and make real the anointing of the Spirit in ourselves; they are the ones whom we have been anointed to anoint. We have been taken from their midst, and we can fearlessly identify with these ordinary people. Each of us has our own story. A little bit of memory will do us much good. They are an image of our soul and an image of the Church. Each of them incarnates the one heart of our people.

We priests are the poor man and we would like to have the heart of the poor widow whenever we give alms, touching the hand of the beggar and looking him or her in the eye. We priests are Bartimaeus, and each morning we get up and pray: "Lord, that I may see." We priests are, in some point of our sinfulness, the man beaten by the robbers. And we want first to be in the compassionate hands of the Good Samaritan, in order then to be able to show compassion to others with our own hands.

I confess to you that whenever I confirm and ordain, I like to smear with chrism the foreheads and the hands of those I anoint. In that generous anointing, we can sense that our own anointing is being renewed. I would say this: We are not distributors of bottled oil. We have been anointed to anoint. We anoint by distributing ourselves, distributing our vocation and our heart. When we anoint others, we ourselves are anointed anew by the faith and the affection of our people. We anoint by dirtying our hands in touching the wounds, the sins and the worries of the people. We anoint by perfuming our hands in touching their faith, their hopes, their fidelity and the unconditional generosity of their self-giving, which many significant figures describe as superstition.

The one who learns how to anoint and to bless is thus healed of meanness, abuse and cruelty.

Let us pray, dear brothers; being with Jesus in the midst of our people is the most beautiful place to be. May the Father *renew deep within us the Spirit of holiness*; may he grant that we be one *in imploring his mercy for the people entrusted to our care and for all the world*. In this way, the multitude of the peoples, gathered in Christ, may become the one faithful people of God, which will attain its fullness in the Kingdom (cf. *Prayer of Priestly Ordination*).

CHAPTER SEVEN

Our Apostolic Closeness

Holy Chrism Mass, Homily of His Holiness Pope Francis,
Vatican Basilica, Holy Thursday, March 29, 2018

Dear brother priests of the Diocese of Rome and other dioceses throughout the world!

When I was reading the texts of today's liturgy, I kept thinking of the passage from Deuteronomy: "For what great nation is there that has a god so near to it as the Lord our God is to us, whenever we call upon him?" (4:7). The closeness of God…our apostolic closeness.

In the reading from the prophet Isaiah, we contemplate the Servant, "anointed and sent" among his people, close to the poor, the sick, the prisoners…and the Spirit who is "upon him," who strengthens and accompanies him on his journey.

In Psalm 88, we see how the closeness of God, who led King David by the hand when he was young, and sustained him as he grew old, takes on the name of fidelity: closeness maintained over time is called fidelity.

The Book of Revelation brings us close to the Lord who always "comes"—[in Greek] *erchómenos*—in person, always. The words "every eye will see him, even those who pierced him" makes us realize that the wounds of the Risen Lord are always visible. The Lord always comes to us, if we choose to draw near, as "neighbors," to the flesh of all those who suffer, especially children.

At the heart of today's Gospel, we see the Lord through the eyes of his own people, which were "fixed on him" (Luke 4:20). Jesus stood up to read in his synagogue in Nazareth. He was given the scroll of the prophet Isaiah. He unrolled it until he found, near the end, the passage about the Servant. He read it aloud: "The Spirit of the Lord is upon me, because he has anointed and sent me…" (Isa 61:1). And he concluded by challenging his hearers to recognize the closeness contained in those words: "Today this Scripture has been fulfilled in your hearing" (Luke 4:21).

Jesus finds the passage and reads it with the proficiency of a scribe. He could have been a scribe or a doctor of the law, but he wanted to be an "evangelizer," a street preacher, the "bearer of joyful news" for his people, the preacher whose feet are beautiful, as Isaiah says. The Preacher is always close.

This is God's great choice: the Lord chose to be close to his people. Thirty years of hidden life! Only then did he begin his preaching. Here we see the pedagogy of the Incarnation, a pedagogy of inculturation, not only in foreign cultures but also in our own parishes, in the new culture of young people…

Closeness is more than the name of a specific virtue; it is an attitude that engages the whole person, our way of relating, our way of being attentive both to ourselves and to others…. When people say of a priest, "he is close to us," they usually mean two things. The first is that "he is always there" (as opposed to never being there: in that case, they always begin by saying, "Father, I know you are very busy..."). The other is that he has a word for everyone. "He talks to everybody," they say, with adults and children alike, with the poor, with those who do not believe....Priests who are "close," available, priests who are there for people, who talk to everyone...street priests.

And one of those who learned from Jesus how to be a street preacher was Philip. In the Acts of the Apostles we read that he went about evangelizing in all the cities and that they were filled with joy (cf. 8:4, 5–8). Philip was one of those whom the Spirit could "seize" at any moment and make him go out to evangelize, moving from place to place, someone capable of even baptizing people of good faith, like the court official of the Queen of the Ethiopians, and doing it right there at the roadside (cf. Acts 8:5, 36–40).

Closeness, dear brothers, is crucial for an evangelizer because it is a key attitude in the Gospel (the Lord uses it to describe his Kingdom). We can be certain that closeness is the key to mercy, for mercy would not be mercy unless, like a Good Samaritan, it finds ways to shorten distances. But I also think we need to realize even more that closeness is also the key to truth; not just the key to mercy, but the key to truth. Can distances really be shortened where truth is concerned? Yes, they can. Because truth is not only the definition of situations and things from a certain distance, by abstract and logical reasoning. It is more than that. Truth is also fidelity ([in Hebrew] *émeth*). It makes you name people with their real name, as the Lord names them, before categorizing them or defining "their situation." There is a distasteful habit, is there not, of following a "culture of the adjective": this is so, this is such and such, this is like... No! This is a child of God. Then come the virtues or defects, but [first] the faithful truth of the person and not the adjective regarded as the substance.

We must be careful not to fall into the temptation of making idols of certain abstract truths. They can be comfortable idols, always within easy reach; they offer a certain prestige and power and are difficult to discern. Because the "truth-idol" imitates, it dresses itself up in the words of the Gospel, but does not let those words touch the heart. Much worse, it distances ordinary people from the healing closeness of the word and of the sacraments of Jesus.

Here, let us turn to Mary, Mother of priests. We can call upon her as "Our Lady of Closeness." "As a true mother, she walks at our side, she shares our struggles and she constantly *surrounds us with God's love*", in such a way that no one feels left out (*Evangelii Gaudium* 286). Our Mother is not only close when she sets out "with haste" to serve, which is one means of closeness, but also by her way of expressing herself (*Ibid.*, 288). At the right moment in Cana, the tone with which she says to the servants, "Do whatever he tells you," will make those words the maternal model of all ecclesial language. But to say those words as she does, we must not only ask her for the grace to do so, but also to be present wherever the important things are "concocted": the important things of each heart, each family, each culture. Only through this kind of closeness— "concocted" in the same way meals are prepared and cooked in a kitchen—can we discern that wine that is missing, and what is the best wine that the Lord wants to provide.

I suggest that you meditate on three areas of priestly closeness where the words, "Do everything Jesus tells you," need to be heard—in a thousand different ways but with the same motherly tone—in the hearts of all those with whom we speak. Those words are "spiritual accompaniment," "confession," and "preaching."

Closeness in spiritual conversation. Let us reflect on this by considering the encounter of the Lord with the Samaritan woman. The Lord teaches her to discern first how to worship, in spirit and in truth. Then, he gently helps her to acknowledge her sin, without offending her. And finally, the Lord infects her with his missionary spirit and goes with her to evangelize her village. The Lord gives us a model of spiritual conversation; he knows how to bring the sin of the Samaritan woman to light without its overshadowing her prayer of adoration or casting doubt on her missionary vocation.

Closeness in confession. Let us reflect on this by considering the passage of the woman caught in adultery. It is clear that here closeness is everything, because the truths of Jesus always approach and can be spoken face to face. Looking the other in the eye, like the Lord, who, after kneeling next to the adulteress about to be stoned, stood up and said to her, "Nor do I condemn you" (John 8:11). This is not to go against the Law. We too can add, "Go and sin no more," not with the legalistic tone of truth as definition—the tone of those who feel that that they have to determine the parameters of divine mercy. On the contrary, those words need to be spoken with the tone of truth as fidelity, to enable the sinner to look ahead and not behind. The right tone of the words "sin no more" is seen in the confessor who speaks them and is willing to repeat them seventy times seven.

Finally, *closeness in preaching.* Let us reflect on this by thinking of those who are far away, and listening to Peter's first sermon, which is part of the Pentecost event. Peter declares that the word is "for all that are far off" (Acts 2:39), and he preaches in such a way that they were "cut to the heart" by the kerygma, which led them to ask: "What shall we do?" (Acts A question, as we said, we must always raise and answer arian and ecclesial tone. The homily is the touchstone "for judging a pastor's closeness and ability to communicate to his people" (*Evangelii Gaudium* 135). In the homily, we can see how close we have been to God in prayer and how close we are to our people in their daily lives.

The good news becomes present when these two forms of closeness nourish and support one another. If you feel far from God, please draw nearer to your people, who will heal you from the ideologies that cool your fervour. The little ones will teach you to look at Jesus in a different way. For in their eyes, the person of Jesus is attractive, his good example has moral authority, his teachings are helpful for the way we live our lives. And if you feel far from people, approach the Lord and his word: in the Gospel, Jesus will teach you his way of looking at people, and how precious in his eyes is every individual for whom he shed his blood on the Cross. In closeness to God, the Word will become flesh in you and you will become a priest close to all flesh. Through your closeness to the people of God, their suffering flesh will speak to your heart and you will be moved to speak to God. You will once again become an intercessory priest.

A priest who is close to his people walks among them with the closeness and tenderness of a good shepherd; in shepherding them, he goes at times before them, at times remains in their midst and at other times walks behind them. Not only do people greatly appreciate such a priest. Even more, th feel that there is something special about him: somethir only feel in the presence of Jesus. That is why disc closeness to them is not simply one more thing either make Jesus present in the life of h remain on the level of ideas, letters or most in some good habit gradually bec

Dear brother priests, let us a Closeness," to bring us closer to o

---